- *The White Museum*

also by George Bilgere

Haywire (Utah State University Press)
The Good Kiss (University of Akron Press)
Big Bang (Copper Beech Press)
The Going (University of Missouri Press)

• *The White Museum*

George Bilgere

Autumn House Press

PITTSBURGH

Autumn House Press Staff
Editor-in-Chief and Founder: Michael Simms
Executive Director: Richard St. John
Community Outreach Director: Michael Wurster
Co-Director: Eva-Maria Simms
Fiction Editor: Sharon Dilworth
Coal Hill Editor: Joshua Storey
Associate Editor: Esther Harder
Fulfillment Manager: Bernadette James
Assistant Editors: Carolyne Whelan, Evan Oare
Editorial Consultant: Ziggy Edwards
Media Consultant: Jan Beatty
Tech Crew Chief: Michael Milberger
Intern: Christina Haaf

This project was supported by the Pennsylvania Council on the Arts, a state agency, through its regional arts funding partnership, Pennsylvania Partners in the Arts (PPA). State government funding comes through an annual appropriation by Pennsylvania's General Assembly. PPA is administered in Allegheny County by Greater Pittsburgh Arts Council.

ISBN: 978-1-932870-35-0
Library of Congress Control Number: 2009939552

- *For Betty*

• *Acknowledgments*

Some of the poems in this collection have appeared in the following journals:

FIELD	"Graduates of Western Military Academy"
Fulcrum	"The Fall," "Shine"
NOR	"Whirlpool," "The Sparrow"
Ploughshares	"Muscle"
River Styx	"Lewis," "Sunset Knoll," "Galileo"
Southwest Review	"Snow"
Whiskey Island	"Owl"

"Sunset Knoll" appeared on Verse Daily.

"Graduates of Western Military Academy" received a 2009 Pushcart Prize.

"Zero," "Bridal Shower," "The Fall," "Snow," "Sunset Knoll," "The White Museum" and "Whirlpool" were broadcast on Garrison Keillor's *The Writer's Almanac*.

I am grateful to John Carroll University and the Ohio Arts Council for their generous support during the writing of this book.

My thanks to Jodie Rufus, John Donoghue, Roger Craik, John McBratney, and Betty Bilgere for their advice, wisdom, and patience.

• *Contents*

Dwells with me still mine irksome Memory,
Which, both to keepe, and lose, grieves equally.

John Donne

one

• *Zero*

First it was five above, then two,
then one morning just plain zero.
There was a strange thrill in saying it.
It's zero, I said,
when you got up.

I was pouring your coffee
and suddenly the whole house made sense:
the roof, the walls, the little heat registers
rattling on the floor. Even the mortgage. Zero,
you said, still in your robe.

And you walked to the window and looked out
at the blanket of snow on the garden
where last summer you planted carrots
and radishes, sweet peas and onions,
and a tiny rainforest of tomatoes
in the hot delirium of June.

Yes, I said, with a certain grim finality,
staring at the white cap of snow on the barbecue grill
I'd neglected to put in the garage for winter.
And the radio says it could go lower.

I like that robe. It's white and shimmery,
and has a habit of falling open
unless you tie it just right.

This wasn't the barbarians at the gate.
It wasn't Carthage in flames, or even
the Donner Party. But it was zero, by God,
and the robe fell open.

• *Bridal Shower*

Perhaps, in a distant café,
four or five people are talking
with the four or five people
who are chatting on their cell phones this morning
in my favorite café.

And perhaps someone there,
someone like me, is watching them as they frown,
or smile, or shrug
to their invisible friends or lovers,
jabbing the air for emphasis.

And, like me, he misses the old days,
when talking to yourself
meant you were crazy,
back when being crazy was a big deal,
not just an acronym
or something you could take a pill for.

I liked it
when people who were talking to themselves
might actually have been talking to God
or an angel.
You respected people like that.

You didn't want to kill them,
as I want to kill the woman at the next table
with the little blue light on her ear
who has been telling the emptiness in front of her
about her daughter's bridal shower
in astonishing detail
for the past thirty minutes.

O person like me,
phoneless in your distant café,
I wish we could meet to discuss this,
and perhaps you would help me
murder this woman on her cell phone,

after which we could have a cup of coffee,
maybe a bagel, and talk to each other,
face to face.

• *Ardmore Tree Service*

My neighbor down the street
works for Ardmore Tree Service.
His truck says it, his shirt says it, there's no
doubt about it. I've seen him
at the grocery store on a summer night,
still in his tree shirt after work,
sap on his hands, bits of leaf in his hair.
He's been in a tree all day,
high above the earth, at home
with the birds and clouds,
lopping this, pruning that, sometimes
feeding a whole tree
to the howling shredder.
Hard work, and I don't begrudge him
the six-pack in his grocery cart
with the pork chops, nor the afterthought
he ran back for: a bunch of daisies
for his wife. I like that,
and am reassured,
pleased with the uniqueness
of our whole species.
Because if the sun blows a fuse,
as it must one day, and we're toast,
I don't think you'll ever see anything
quite like this again—trees and clouds,
maybe, and even rain and lightning bugs
on August nights. But
I don't see the six-pack, the tall cool ones
with a picture of a mountain lake on the label,
nor Ardmore Tree Service, nor
the gift of the daisies, presented dripping
in their clear plastic sheath, ever
quite happening again.

• *Graduates of Western Military Academy*

One day, as this friend of my father, Paul,
was flying over Asia,
he vaporized a major Japanese city.

True story. They'd been chums
at a military academy in Illinois
back in the thirties.

My father was the star: best in Latin,
best in riflery and history,
best in something called "recitation,"

and best at looking serious.
In the old yearbooks he has exactly the look
you were supposed to have back then:
about fifty-two percent duty, forty-eight percent integrity.
Zero percent irony.

But somehow, all my father got to do later on
was run his own car dealership. A big one,
but still. While Paul
got to blow up Japan. My father
ushered in the latest models.
Paul ushered in the Atomic Age.
It seems unfair, but there you are.

Paul had been an indifferent Latin scholar. Weak
in history and recitation. For these and other reasons
My father took a refreshing swim
across a large, inviting lake of gin,
complete with strange boats and exotic shore birds,

which resulted in his interment
under some shady acres I occasionally visit.

While Paul went on for decades,
always giving the same old speech. Yes,
he'd done the right thing. No doubt about it.

He improved his skills at recitation
and developed a taste for banquet food.
To this day he struggles with his weight.

• *Snow*

A heavy snow, and men my age
  all over the city
are having heart attacks in their driveways,

dropping their nice new shovels
  with the ergonomic handles
that finally did them no good.

Gray-headed men who meant no harm,
  who abided by the rules and worked hard
for modest rewards, are slipping

softly from their mortgages,
  falling out of their marriages.
How gracefully they swoon—

that lovely, old-fashioned word—
  from grandkids, pension plans,
vacations in Florida.

They should have known better
  than to shovel snow at their age.
If only they'd heeded

the sensible advice of their wives
  and hired a snow-removal service.
But there's more to life

than merely being sensible. Sometimes
  a man must take up his shovel
and head out alone into the snow.

• *The Fall*

Although there were no witnesses
in the hallway outside the woman's room
of the Hotel Coronado,
when my aunt stumbled
and fell to her knees on the ancient marble,

it must have been like the swordsman
falling in *The Seven Samurai,*
a whole dynasty collapsing,
falling out of its bones
into the mud. I was reading
the sports section in the lobby
when a boy, probably sixteen or so,
ran in and called my name.
An old woman has fallen,
he said, frightened that something
so enormous could happen, that fate
should cast him as an emissary
announcing dynastic collapse
instead of just a high school kid,

and I stood up and ran to her
although I'm fifty-six now, and breaking
into a spontaneous run feels like
trying out a first language you'd lost
as a kid who swapped countries.

And there she sat, lean and elegant,
like an athlete who'd collapsed
from sheer exhaustion, her legs
drawn up to her chin as she fought
to lift the whole city again,

the crumbling Coronado,
where Miles Davis used to play,
and the Continental, where the Gershwins
hung out at the Tack Room,
and the abandoned Fox Theater
where she saw Olivier's *Hamlet*,

and even the boarded up
Forest Park Boat House, where her father
used to take her for ice cream
in the sweltering summers.

An old woman has fallen.

• *Ash Borers*

The ash borers! Here's what I like about them:
They have no hidden agenda.
They just want to bore, ash
in particular. Into the big old boles
they drive their ugly faces.
These are trees, you understand,
that have stood here for a century.
Whole dynasties of kids
have spent their summers beneath them.
So no love is lost for the ash borer,
even though no one has ever seen one
(except on TV, highly magnified, last night).
And odd that we don't really see the trees,
the simple giants watching over us,
until one turns up missing. Then
that sudden hole in the upper right-
hand corner of the windshield
shocks you on the drive home with the power
of Nothing. You remember how strong
the tree was, how it held you in its arms.
But it's not coming back. Ever. And each day
the sky is a little larger, thanks
to the ash borer. The tree men come
with their chain saws and chippers.
Their rough-hewn surgery
leaves us naked in the sun,
and the ash borers move on,
unpunished, unrepentant, to bore
another town's heaven,
to ravish its history,
to kill, for God knows what reasons,
the ash tree.

• *Laundry Chute*

In go the dirty socks and underwear,
last week's stale shirts. The slacks
with their drizzle of bisque.

It's so easy
that while I'm at it
I throw in the car's old brakes
and the weird new sound
the fridge has started to make,

along with that nasty crack of my father's
from last night's nightmare. And the fact
that I can't quite manage to unremember
what I didn't manage to say to my mother
the last time we ever saw each other.

Into the black hole
go the lies I've told, the big ones
that certain people I love
still carry around like wounds.
And something I'd rather not mention
involving a couple of women
and a lot of gin.

Meanwhile, far beneath me,
the steady, reassuring hum
of subterranean machinery.

I've got a few days
before everything finds its way back up,
cleaned, pressed, and folded.

• *Sparrow*

On the bricks of the patio
a sparrow is struggling with a used tampon
it half-flew, half-dragged here
from a dumpster across the street.

The tampon resembles a wounded rat.
Those of us enjoying our coffee
and *New York Times* in the spring morning
pretend to ignore it.

But all the suns in all the galaxies,
and all the planets around our own paltry star,
are turning on the same invisible pulleys
that drive the sparrow
to build a cozy little crib
in the eaves under somebody's gutters,

and to find, sooner the better,
another sparrow who hears
the same music of the spheres.

You can't argue with that.

And though some of us on the patio might believe
that what the sparrow is wrestling with
is the blight man was born for,
the curse Adam fell for,

for the bird
it's an engineering problem: the tampon's
too stubbornly stitched together
for a tiny beak to tear apart,

and too heavy
with human blood to carry off
into the blue air of the future.

• *Shine*

The sweet blonde coed, in bondage
to the little gold tennis chain on her ankle,
drops her fruit salad all over the floor
and says to her friend,
I'm, like, a total spazz,

and a middle-aged black woman
in the livery of the University Food Services
hustles out to clean it up.

And that, folks, is the way it is.

I have a friend who brings along an extra pair of shoes
whenever he flies,
so the last remaining shoeshine boy in America,
gray-headed and smiling,
can give them a little spit and polish
in Terminal B of the Cleveland Airport.

And I'd love to see Larry,
tenured professor in the business department,
wine expert and golfer, with his back issues
of *Forbes* and *Conde Nast Traveler*
in a neat pile beside his toilet,

kneeling at the feet of a black man,
trying to raise a shine, his own
reflection, from the scarred black face
of history.

He'd have a theory, a graph,
a PowerPoint presentation
for why it all turned out this way,
for why some poor tech-support nerd in Duluth
lost his job last month
to some poor tech-support nerd in Calcutta

who has to pick his way down an alley
full of malarial strays
to answer the phone for Bill Gates
and explain to Larry

why his program isn't running,
his numbers aren't crunching,
why the great March of Progress is being held back,
making him twenty minutes late
to the driving range,

where he envisions himself
as Tiger Woods,
frightening the white folk at Augusta
with his booming drives,

a miracle of the imagination
no less strange

than the fact that we are friends
who will sit down tonight at our table
at La Dolce Vita, where Larry will put aside
his distressed leather valise
full of self-serving conservative bullshit,

and I will push aside
my battered canvas Peace Corps backpack
full of high-minded liberal bullshit,

and we will eat of the cow
and drink of the grape
while the tv sputters with madness above us

and the herds of beautiful women,
seeing that we are feeding, and therefore
not dangerous,
graze indifferently beside us.

- *Doggy Dip*

Each year in our town,
after the public pool
has had its last sad day of summer,
and the umbrellas have been folded
and the gods and goddesses have come down
from their lifeguard chairs,
we hold the annual Doggy Dip.

For once the gate of heaven,
with its NO DOGS sign, is open
to our local beagles
and boxers, our setters and spaniels,
our snooty pugs, and tough,
blue-collar shepherds,
and the whole furry cacophony
of mutts and mixes and mongrels.

Every nation has its holy days,
its resurrections and atonements,
its feasts and fasts, its gloomy penitents
flogging themselves bloody
on even the nicest afternoons.

Give me the Doggy Dip any day,
the public waters churning
with happy pooches, purified and absolved
of all their doggy sins, ready
for another year of biting
the postman, peeing on the rug,

howling in the middle of the night
at something we can no longer see,
or hear, or even remember.

- *View from the Deck*

The backyard is moving so fast
through summer I can see the breeze
registered by the seismic tips
of the honeysuckle. I am having a beer
as we dip over the horizon. To the left
I can hear my neighbor watering
her perennials, off in the country
of cancer, just beyond the hedge.

Her snapdragons glisten by cancer-light,
the finches at her feeder
are cancer-lovely, and even the tilting
garage, paint peeling in the dusk, glows
with the cancerous beauty of old garages.

Nice evening, she calls to me
in cancer, a language I learned
from my mother, who spoke it
beautifully. The beer is very cold,
and a sycamore at the yard's edge
is coming apart in the twilight.

The sprinkler bends to silver
the primrose, stands straight up,
then goes down for another look. Yes,
I say, in my perfectly inflected cancer,
and tomorrow's supposed to be
even nicer.

• *The White Museum*

My aunt was an organ donor
and so, the day she died,
her organs were harvested
for medical science.

I suppose there must be people
who list, under "Occupation,"
"Organ Harvester," people for whom
it is always harvest season,
each death bringing its bounty.
They spend their days
loading wagonloads of kidneys,
whole cornucopias of corneas,
burlap sacks groaning with hearts and lungs
and the pale green sprouts of gall bladders,
and even, from time to time,
the weighty cauliflower of a brain.

And perhaps today,
as I sit in this café, watching the snow
and thinking about my aunt,
a young medical student somewhere
is moving through the white museum
of her brain, making his way slowly
from one great room to the next.

Here is the gallery of her girlhood,
with that great canvas depicting her father
holding her on his lap in the backyard
of their bungalow in St. Louis.

And here is a sketch of her
the summer after her mother died,
walking down a street in Berlin
when the broken city was itself
a museum. And here

is a small, vivid oil of the two of us
sitting in a café in London
arguing over the work of Constable
or Turner, or Francis Bacon
after a visit to the Tate.

I want you to know, as you sit there
with your microscope and your slides,
there's no need to be reverent before these images.
That's the last thing she would have wanted.
But do be respectful. Speak quietly.
No flash photography. Tell your friends
you saw something beautiful.

• *Whirlpool*

In the morning, after much delay,
I finally go down to the basement
to replace the broken dryer belt.

First, I unbolt the panels
and sweep up the dust mice and crumbling spiders.
I listen to the sounds of the furnace
thinking things over
at the beginning of winter.

Then I stretch out on the concrete floor
with a flashlight in my mouth
to contemplate the mystery
of the tensioner-pulley assembly.

And finally, with a small, keen pleasure,
I slip the new belt over the spindle, rise,
and screw everything back together.

Later, we have Thanksgiving dinner
with my wife's grandmother, who is dying
of bone cancer. Maybe,
if they dial up the chemo, fine tune the meds,
we'll do this again next year.

But she's old, and the cancer
seems to know what it's doing.
Everyone loves her broccoli casserole.
As for the turkey, it sits on the table,
a small, brown mountain we can't see beyond.

That night I empty the washer,
throw the damp clothes into the dryer.
For half-an-hour my wife's blouses
wrestle with my shirts
in a hot and whirling ecstasy,

because I replaced an ancient belt
and adjusted the tensioner-pulley assembly.

• *Trash*

> Each morning I place on my writing table
> a carnation and a hammer.
> *Neruda*

In fifth grade, I think it was, or even sixth,
the teacher got so fed up
with the trash stuffed into my desk,
she made me dump it out on the floor
in front of the whole classroom.
And there, amidst the detritus
I'd spent the spring collecting
on my one-mile morning walk
to Lowell Elementary—the lost keys
and toy soldiers, the scraps of smut,
the pencil stubs and broken protractors,
my half-eaten peanut butter sandwiches—
was a dead bird and a pink garter belt.
This from a time when folk still walked,
when the sidewalks were peopled
with travelers, when Fuller Brush men
and encyclopedia salesmen, and blind
sellers of brooms still walked the earth.
When every morning I left the house
in my blue Dodgers jacket, my eyes
peeled for odd stuff along the way,
like the sparrow, mummified
in the dry California air, flightless
and silent on the mica-glitter
of the sidewalk. And the garter belt,
balled up in some ivy. I didn't know
what to make of it, only that the silver
hooks meant to catch the invisible
waist of girl—a girl not my mother—
frightened me, like the empty
little talons of the sparrow, curled
around death. Mrs. Eicker turned red

and made me throw all of it—sparrow,
garter belt, rotting sandwiches,
the wads and clumps—in the trash,
although nothing is ever really lost.

- *Blank*

When I came to my mother's house
the day after she had died
it was already a museum of her
unfinished gestures. The mysteries
from the public library, due
in two weeks. The half-eaten square
of lasagna in the fridge.

The half-burned wreckage
of her last cigarette,
and one red swallow
of wine in a lipsticked
glass beside her chair.

Finally, a blue Bic
on a couple of downs
and acrosses left blank
in the Sunday crossword,
which actually had the audacity
to look a little smug
at having, for once, won.

• *Sunset Knoll*

When the smoking hot barista
  pushes my toasted bagel across the counter to me
without so much as a glance

because all her pistils and stamens and sweet
  pink petals are on orange alert
for the punker next to me, Armageddon
  tattooed on his arms, and furthermore

she's even forgotten the cream cheese
  because I've reached the age
when I'm, like, totally invisible to her,

I briefly consider
  picking up the plate and smashing it
through the countertop, sending a rain
  of glass onto the tea biscuits and cinnamon scones.

That'd show her, all right.

Then I remember
  my summer as a feeder

in that nursing home back in L.A.,
  spooning whipped ham into the mouth-holes
of those bedridden husks of paper maché.

How sometimes the old guys would pull out
  their dentures and throw them across the room
just for the hell of it, just to remind me
  I'm still here, you little shit.

So,

  Thanks, I say
and walk back to my table.

  Like I needed the cream cheese anyway.

• *Writers' Conference*

On the last night
we sat around on the deck
near the hot tub, the moon getting weirder
with every margarita.

And one of the women in the workshop,
who wrote tough little elegies
for her marriage, said that reading
this particular Irish poet
could make her climax.

And another woman,
a compact blonde who did *tai chi* every morning
and wrote poems about loneliness
being the bed her husband left her, said,

a good poem *is* an orgasm; it's the language
touching its own body
until it comes. And I knew

it was just a matter of time
before somebody slipped out of her bra
and Birkenstocks,
road-weary yet encouraged
by moonlight and tequila.

We were about to have an *experience*

we were all too old for,
something that in the light of morning
would look like the headless little mouse
the cat leaves beside you on the pillow
as a gift. Or a warning.

I said something
about how late it was getting,
and the spell broke
with a small, embarrassed pop.

Mine was the voice of reason,
of bland middle-age,
although I knew perfectly well

it would have been a different story
if Jennifer, the willowy grad student
from the local agricultural college
they'd given me as an assistant that week
had risen in her underwear
from that hot pool of moonfoam…

But I'm afraid
the days of my Jennifers have passed.

I'm entering a new season:
season of elegies
and minor hypocrisies.

- *Muscle*

One minute
  I'm standing in the parking lot
behind the De Anza theater. We're throwing our empties

at each other, our smokes turning a whiter
  shade of pale.
The subject is horsepower,

  and the cars we're leaning on
are Cougars,
    Mustangs, GTOs.

  Now and then we rumble off
and back again
  for no particular reason.

Just to hear the anger, *basso profundo*,
  from a 389 V8, as rendered
by a righteous pair of Hooker headers.

When suddenly,
  through a dirty, underhanded
trick of time, I'm turning gray

at a table in front of Starbuck's.
  Sipping a latte, talking mortgage
with a woman I seem to be married to.

A silly little Prius
  scoots by without a sound,
followed by a bleak Insight.

• *Rhino*

It seems like only yesterday that I saw one,
with its prissy, fat-lady-in-heels sashay,
bearing its fabled horn, its namesake.

But a friend of mine, against my advice,
recently underwent rhinoplasty,

and the next time I saw her,
with her perfect little high-tech nose,
I realized I could barely remember
the last time I'd been to the zoo.

One day long ago
I walked out of the elephant house forever,
leaving behind its ineffable stench of elephant.

And I walked out of the primate correctional facility
full of chimps shouting,
J'accuse.

And I stood for the last time
in front of the rhino enclosure,
where the rhino lay in the dust and boredom,
her little gray tail whisking at flies.

That was the last time I can remember
holding the big, extinct paw
of my father as we walked out of the zoo together,
filled with the autumnal sadness of zoos.

It's the way I feel
when I bump into Kate these days. Like the rhino
remembering the Serengeti.
Or like seeing someone I used to know.

• *Pasta Fasul*

A dark-haired young woman, maybe eighteen,
is striding across the campus
toward an elegant, Tudor-style house with a curving driveway.

A couple of kids are inside,
the boy struggling with Chopin, the girl
wrestling with a cocker spaniel.
They're waiting for the sound of Daddy's car,
back from his office downtown.

And she'd like to get home in time
to have dinner ready, but it doesn't seem likely.

So they'll probably end up going out
to Mario's, on the Hill,

which suddenly sounds pretty good.
Maybe the gnocchi this time, and some wine,
or not the gnocchi but the pasta fasul.
But still, the wine.

In any case, it's nice
being married to a lawyer. No—a doctor.
She hasn't decided yet. That's still
a few years down the line.

• *The Ineffable*

I'm sitting here reading the paper,
feeling warm and satisfied, basically content
with my life and all I have achieved.
Then I go up for a refill and suddenly realize
how much happier I could be with the barista.
Late thirties, hennaed hair, an ahnk
or something tattooed on her ankle,
a little silver ring in her nostril.
There's some mystery surrounding why she's here,
pouring coffee and toasting bagels at her age.
But there's a lot of torsion when she walks,
which is interesting. I can sense right away
how it would all work out between us.

We'd get a loft in the artsy part of town,
and I can see how we'd look shopping together
at our favorite organic market
on a snowy winter Saturday,
snowflakes in our hair,
our arms full of leeks and shiitake mushrooms.
We would do *tai chi* in the park.
She'd be one of the few people
who actually "gets" my poetry
which I'd read to her in bed.
And I can see us making love, by candlelight,
struggling to find words for the ineffable.
We never dreamed it could be like this.

And it would all be great, for many months,
until one day, unable to help myself,
I'd say something about that nostril ring.
Like, do you really need to wear that tonight
at Sarah and Mike's house, Sarah and Mike being
pediatricians who intimidate me slightly
with their patrician cool, and serious money.

And she would give me a look,
a certain lifting of the eyebrows
I can see she's capable of, and right there
that would be the end of the ineffable.

• *Lewis*

When my wife told me she was having an affair
I stormed out of the house
and lived for a week in my office,
too hurt and bewildered to go back home,
too cheap to pay for a hotel.

And on the seventh night
as I lay on the floor, drunk and passed out
under my windbreaker, I heard Lewis,
the janitor, opening the door
to empty my trash can.

But I was in the middle of a strange dream
about being caught by an indignant woman
while peeing in the women's bathroom
during an emergency in the public library.

So as the doorknob was turning
and I was about to be discovered
on the office floor in my underwear,
I shouted in my confusion,

Why don't you go pee in the men's room,
see what it's like, and we'll call it even—

and from the other side of the door
I heard Lewis, a fine and courteous man
I have known for many years, say,

Ok, Professor. You have yourself a pleasant evening.

But how could I.

- *Americana*

Although what I'd planned to accomplish today
was the final draft of the annual department evaluation
due last month,

what I'm actually going to do
is get on my ten-speed
and roll through the late August afternoon,
the dreaming neighborhoods
with their sprinklers and ancient trees and ceramic trolls,
down to the public pool.

I will swim a few lazy laps
beneath the stupendous clouds
shape-shifting above me,
and practice saying *chaise longue*
while enjoying the light-speed impact
of the sun on my shoulders.

I will do nothing
but listen to the mysterious tongues
of children,
the whispered yearnings of the mothers.
I will think of my father, dead
forty years ago today,
and stare at the breasts
of that sixteen-year-old girl
in the sky-colored bikini. Touching them
would mean the electric chair,
but still…

In any case, it's not the sort of thought
my father would have entertained
in his dark suit and wingtips,
nor my grandfather, in his dark suit and wingtips,
as they built the soaring skyline
of the last century.

They saw some amazing things in their day—
the Great War, the Depression, the Bomb—

but nothing like the spectacle
of a man my age
wearing a faded Target swimsuit
made in a Chinese sweatshop,
hanging out at the public pool,
scoping out some hot teen boobs
in the middle of the day,
smack dab in the middle of the work week.

Yes, dad, I know
I'm living in a minor key,

a minor age, you'd probably say. I failed
to grow up. Perhaps you'd find it
pathetic, but I like it here
in this unimaginable future
you never lived to see,

this dress down, come-as-you-are,
hey-it's-no-big-deal kind of a place,

where I have no further plans,
other than stopping at the DQ
for a soft-cone dipped in chocolate,
a sweet elegy for summer,

melting in the afternoon
as fast as I can eat it
before I pedal away,
taking the long way home.

• *Bike Show: Dayton, Ohio*

The men walk around smoking,
checking out the bikes. The women
walk around with the men, some
looking reasonably hot.

The women don't give a damn
about the bikes. They size up
each other, assess the competition,
or just stare off vacantly into the distances,
waiting to leave.

Then they climb on board
behind the guy they came with.
They tuck themselves onto that little perch
and roar off in the heat and wind.

Hard to know why they do this.
I'm guessing it's a negotiation.
The poor guys with their muscles
and Freedom Riders vests,
their tattoos and their Skoal,

haven't figured out
that two, maybe three years, the woman
will hold on for dear life back there.

Then he damn well better come through
with ring-house-kid.
Trade in the roar
of his straight-pipe Harley
for a riding mower.

Or she'll park her sweet ass on the back
of somebody else's id.

• *Roses*

A late fall day, and unseasonably warm enough,
for whatever dire reasons,
to let me paint the rose trellis

a deep red in the brittle afternoon,
enjoying the gratitude of thirsty old wood
soaking up the blood.

This is satisfying,
for some reason, although I realize

that somewhere an aging surgeon
is stepping out for a showdown
with a famous young tumor
on the dusty street of somebody's life.

And somewhere else a soldier
is burning in his Hummer,

and a girl in a border town
is strapping a bomb
to the shy breasts
nobody ever got to kiss
before she heads to the marketplace
to mingle with the pears and radishes,
the fish staring from their beds of ice.

But I'm just painting a trellis,
thinking already of the praise I'll get for it,
even though I'm doing my usual half-assed job,
slopping red on the driveway,
Pollocking the flagstones, willing to fall
a little short of perfection,

although I know that spring, when it comes
uttering roses, will settle
for nothing less.

• *Grecian Temples*

Because I'm getting pretty gray at the temples,
which negatively impacts my earning potential
and does not necessarily attract vibrant young women
with their perfumed bosoms to dally with me
on the green hillside,
I go out and buy some Grecian Hair Formula.

And after the whole process, which involves
rubber gloves, a tiny chemistry set,
and perfect timing, I look great.
I look very fresh and virile, full of earning potential.
But when I take my fifteen-year-old beagle
out for his evening walk, the contrast is unfortunate.
Next to me he doesn't look all that great,
with his graying snout, his sort of faded,
worn-out-dog look. It makes me feel old,
walking around with a dog like that.

It's not something a potential employer,
much less a vibrant young woman with a perfumed bosom
would necessarily go for. So I go out
and get some more Grecian Hair Formula—
Light Brown, my beagle's original color.
And after all the rigmarole he looks terrific.
I mean, he's not going to win any friskiness contests,
not at fifteen. But there's a definite visual improvement.
The two of us walk virilely around the block.

The next day a striking young woman at the bookstore
happens to ask me about my parents,
who are, in fact, long dead, due to the effects of age.
They were very old, which causes death.
But having dead old parents does not go
with my virile, intensely fresh new look.

So I say to the woman, my parents are fine.
They love their active lifestyle in San Diego.
You know, windsurfing, jai alai, a still-vibrant sex life.
And while this does not necessarily cause her
to come dally with me on the green hillside, I can tell
it doesn't exactly hurt my chances.

I can see her imagining dinner
with my sparkly, young-seeming mom and dad
at some beachside restaurant
where we would announce our engagement.

Your son has great earning potential,
she'd say to dad, who would take
a gander at her perfumed bosom
and give me a wink, like he used to do
back when he was alive, and vibrant.

• *La Strada*

A dollar got you a folding chair
in the drafty lecture hall
with a handful of other lonely grad students.

Then the big reels and low-tech clatter
of a sixteen-millimeter projector.

Rashomon. HMS Potemkin.
La Belle et la Bête, before
Disney got his hands on it.

And *The Bicycle Thief*, and for God's sake,
La Strada.

You can't find them
at Blockbuster anymore. Only the latest
G-rated animated pixilated computer-generated prequels.

That's just the way it goes.

Even if you could,
you'd see them on DVD,
restored, colorized, scratch-free,
on a plasma-screen TV. With your wife,
your dog, your degree. You'd get up
to answer the phone, check on the baby.

You're just not young enough,
or poor enough, or miserable
enough anymore to see—really *see*

Les Enfants du Paradis, or *Ikiru*,
or *The 400 Blows*. Or, for God's sake,
La Strada.

• *Post-Toccata*

Someone died and left me all this Mozart,
literally a hundred albums, possibly more,
an entire shelf of glittering arpeggios,
and now and then I feel I must sit down
with a glass of wine and listen to a toccata.

While doing this I feel important and even noble
on various levels. Others are listening to Josh Groban
or Madonna at some crowded Starbuck's,
while I sit alone with my toccata,
immersed in the genius of Mozart,
whose fate was to die tragically young and forgotten.

I try to imagine him in his wig and white stockings,
sitting at his klavier, producing glittering arpeggios
as grim Death approaches. Death the Silencer.
Death who silenced my friend, bequeathing me
in excess of one hundred Mozart albums
which all sound kind of the same.

And then, in the midst of a particularly long arpeggio,
or possibly a glissando,
I begin to resent Mozart's implicit assumption
that his thoughts in the face of Death the Silencer
are worthier of being written down—or listened to— than mine;
that his role is to sit at his klavier in his wig,
writing courageous toccatas against oblivion,
while mine is merely to sit on the bleachers and applaud.

The fact is, I've got my own worries about dying tragically forgotten
and (somewhat) young. I'm sitting here sacrificing what time
  remains to me
in order to listen to him go on and on with his endless glissandos.

And such is my resentment that I turn off the record player
and take a long walk around the neighborhood,
brooding about time and loss and the grim approach of inevitable death
at an effectively high aesthetic level.

• *The Bow*

In a corner of the attic, my old bow,
dusty and unstrung.

Last time I used it I'd never heard
of Telemachus or his lost father.
And I was lousy at whittling,
animal husbandry, knots,
and every other skill of scouting.
But I was an archer to be reckoned with.

Watching the bright feathers
rise and head for home
in the distant bale of gold
actually pierced my soul.
Proving that I had one.

Mr. Livermore, the scoutmaster,
really thought it was something.
But he already had a kid.

That boy sure can handle a bow,
he once said, and I just opened up
a secret compartment that came with me
as standard equipment,
took that comment of his
and tucked it away.

• *The First Breast*

I encountered it
in the summer of 1969.
Probably around 10 at night.

This girl and I
were on a bench at Fairmont Park
under the moon.

I felt the conditions were propitious
in that we were both 17
and we had been kissing our way toward this
for about a month.

Furthermore, the night was warm
and smelled of lilacs.

Singlehandedly
I cracked the Braille
of her bra. On Earth
it was perfectly quiet.

Into my palm
came the great hot weight.
It was all so Ptolemaic.

In a week
some men would set down
on the moon.

They clomped around for awhile
on the pale softness,
and left.
But things would never be the same.

• *Below the Rim*

Ants are hard at work
on the cicada at my feet.
It looks like the scorched husk
of a Humvee
swarming with insurgents,

a simile
which is about as close to the war
as I'm likely to get
unless somebody's shampoo blows up
my flight tomorrow, and I fall
in a sticky rain over Kansas,

where Intelligent Design is the hottest thing
since the Old Testament, where now and then
a coffin comes home

and a slumbering farm town breaks
into little explosions
of flags and roses.

One of my students
is spending a few weeks there,
back home in the cornfields,

before shipping out to Baghdad.
We all got a box in the sand
waiting for us, is the reason

he gave me for signing up last May,
and I was too stunned by the phrase,
this former offensive lineman's
borrowed eloquence, to tell him

how full of shit I thought he was,
how stupidly young
and in love with the thought of his doomed beauty.

And besides,
I was remembering Vietnam,
how my stomach shriveled,
how the yellow acid

seeped through my guts
as I watched the Tet Offensive
on the 6 o'clock news in the numb weeks
before my college deferment came through.

And so I said to the kid, whose grade
in my American Authors course
was a kind-hearted C,

Good luck to you then, feeling both
ridiculously old—the graying teacher
sending the young warrior to battle—
and simply ridiculous, for he was heading to Baghdad
and his box,

and I was heading over to the school gym
for a pick-up basketball game
with some other old guys
who gather there in the summer evenings,

still in love
with the smell of varnish and sweat,
the ancient insults, the give and take,

as we play our games, our elegies
for our own lost beauty,
with a cautious, measured devotion,
well below the rim.

three

• *Taking Out the Trash*

I remember as a child
watching my father take out the trash
at the frozen crack of dawn, cursing
as he dragged the stinking cans to the curb,
and thinking, that's not something
I'm ever going to do.

In other ways I was a model son,
standing at the mirror as he shaved,
dabbing the warm cream on my cheek,
dreaming of a razor
and whiskers of my very own.

Watching him light up
as he read the Sunday paper,
one eye squinted against smoke
and bad news, had me reading the funnies
before I could even read, my eye
squinted against nothing.

And the deft, one-handed way
he straightened his fedora's brim,
while at the same time
adjusting the coordinates
of rake and tilt,
makes me regret that the hat,
like my father, has vanished,

along with the strop and razor,
and lathery bowl of curds.
Even smoking, and the Sunday paper
are on their way out.

These are the losses I'm mourning
this morning as I drag the stinking
trash cans to the curb.

• *Greatness*

Monet came in from the cold,
stomping his boots and shaking off the snow.
He was in his haystack period
and he was working on the haystack of winter,
which was proving to be much harder than the haystack of fall.

That one had been easy. The mellow afternoons
turning cool with a hint of wood smoke at twilight.
The ducks coming low over the wheat stubble.
But now his hands and feet, even his paints, were frozen.
However, he was great—a great painter,
the inventor of Impressionism—
which was a consolation.

Alice took his coat, unlaced his boots,
and sat him down at the dinner table.
She knew what was coming: a long talk about the haystack
over wine and her *coq au vin*. She thought,
I eat my suppers with a man who spends his days
staring at a haystack. Week after week. Month after month.
She loved him for his passion,
his steady, bulldog fidelity, but sometimes
she felt a twinge of jealousy toward the haystack.

Soon it would be spring, and Monet
would be painting the haystack of spring. She sighed,
a mixture of contentment and restlessness.
The funny thing was, her *coq au vin*,
on the scale of greatness, was actually superior
to his haystack paintings. Alice was a genius
of the *coq au vin*, and also of the *crêpe*.
Her *crêpes* were miracles, levitating above the plate.

Finally, she had a way of tossing her hair
away from her high, pale forehead
while at the same time
scrunching her lips into a little *moue*,
and she could do this better than any woman in Giverny—
indeed, better than any woman in all of France.

But Greatness, historically speaking, does not concern itself
with *coq au vin* or hair-tossing,
or even that irresistible little *moue*. Greatness, in this case,
is the steady haystack of a man's love,
burning, freezing, coalescing,
but enduring
in the changing light.

• *Owl*

I walk through the eucalyptus grove at dusk,
the best time to see them,
just after the sun has fizzled out in the bay.
And there, on a low branch,

is a Great Horned Owl. *Bubo Virginianus*
Fat as a fire hydrant, fog lamps for eyes.
Owlishly regarding me.

But no. Not really.

There is no owl. There is never
an owl. No one's seen an owl
in these parts for years.
This is an owl-free zone,
it's all owled out, it's been thoroughly
de-owled.

I just wanted an excuse to say
owl,
which, as you know, happens to be
among the top five or ten words
in the English language. *Owl.*

Wolf
is on that list as well, and stuffed
versions of long-gone wolves
can be seen in our local museum.

So, as a community service, I stand
in the owlless woods, within earshot
of the Pacific Coast Highway,
softly whispering *owl.*
Crying *wolf.*

• *A Nice Place to Live*

This summer, as the missiles went back and forth
between the one sobbing angry country and the other,
I went from the shallow end to the deep end,
my evening laps at the public pool,

wondering if there was something wrong with me
for not hating anyone that much.

Not the guy in the Hummer
who cut me off at the exit yesterday,
then gave me the finger.

Not my father, even in my worst moments.
Not even my ex-wife.
I'm a hater from the bush leagues, a small-time hater,

although I have, it's true, gotten myself
through some long patches of self-pity
more or less on hatred alone.

Then I forget. Lose interest.
It's called being white
and well-off in America,
where it's all just handed to you
by a nice brown server with no English,
or a white person with bad teeth
and no dental plan.

And the gravy train is just so smooth
that when the big ideas—the ones
you would have died for, or even killed for,
the ones that take root and flower
only in the harshest desert climes,

wither inside you and die and turn to little figs
at the edge of your plate,
and you don't even like figs—

then it's time for a stroll down to Murphy's
and a couple of beers with Roger
under the evening news.

And tonight it's a weeping bearded man
holding the tailfin of a rocket
that killed his son,

a rocket made by all of us
sitting here at the bar tonight
waiting to turn it to the Indians game.

Nice people, basically.
We don't even bother to hate him.

- *Alleged*

On the way to school this morning
some kids found the body of an intruder.

He'd been intruding in someone's home,
specifically, in their valuables,
when a shot fired by the alleged homeowner
intruded upon the intruder.

At this point
the intruder terminated his intruding,
police said.

He exited the premises in favor of a new venue
which was an alley,
shortly after which death intruded.
Death the intruder.

The shot-intruded intruder
was discovered by the alleged kids
in a state of deceasement,
police said.

The kids were in pursuit
of their educational goals
at Thomas Jefferson High School,
according to witnesses.

They paused to intrude
upon the slain and twice-intruded upon
intruder's pockets,

which contained cash and controlled substances,
for which they were arrested
and are awaiting trial,
police said.

• *Vermeer*

In Vermeer's *Woman with Pregnant Cat*
it is not the light
so much as the absence of light
that darkens the cat's shadow.

Even the shadow is pregnant,
swollen with shadow kitties.

The woman has been eating the bread
that is sitting on the table. Half a loaf
remains. Once again I wonder
at the simplicity of life in those days.
Why bother with a plate? Just put the bread
on the table, assuming the table
is reasonably clean, and get on with it.

The women in Vermeer
always sit by an open window,
and this girl is no exception.
Nothing much is going on outside,
nor inside, for that matter.
She's just kind of staring off into space.
The light from the open window
gives everything that great Dutch look.

Maybe she'll just help herself
to another piece of that bread.

Once I had a cat
that looked exactly like the one she's holding
(like most cats, it eventually got run over).

I think of Vermeer
finishing off this painting, then going out
to a little Delft tavern

and having a beer and a cigar
in his light blue waistcoat,
alone at his table,
at peace with the world,
looking very much like a Vermeer.

• *Joy*

Today I sit on the sun porch
with my body, just the two of us
for a change, the flu
having left me for someone else.

I'm thinking about how good it is
to have been sick, to have been turned
inside out. *Until we are sick*, says Keats,
we understand not. And for four or five days
I understood. Fully and completely.
There was absolutely no ambiguity,
no misunderstandings of any sort whatsoever.

For awhile I thought I'd never get better.
I'd be that sick eagle, staring at the sky
on a permanent basis. But
we're living in the age of miracles:
another jetliner smacked into New York,
only this time nobody got hurt. A black guy
thoroughly fumigated the White House.

And this morning I woke up
feeling like a little French village
the Nazis suddenly decided to pull out of
after a particularly cruel occupation.

The baker has come back to his store
and everything smells like warm baguettes.
The children are playing in the schoolyard,
the piano bars along the river
have thrown open their doors.

And here you are, with coffee
and an open blouse, and two cool breasts
from the land of joy.

• *Father's Day*

As usual, we don't know what to say to each other.

I haven't dropped by for years
and the stones are tilted and disreputable-looking.
The graveyard itself is dying.

It would be nice to sing something,
some Bach or Brahms. His voice,
after all, trained for oratorio and lieder,
is nearly all of him I can remember:
Bist Du Bei Mir echoing from the shower.
But I'm no singer.

Then that little flash of horror—he's alone
in an old suit, a rotten belt, two shoes
he never walked in. He's a box of bones,
all by himself down there.

So I lie down
on the uncut grass above him,
the live bones floating above the dead,

and for twenty minutes or so I gaze up
through the trees at the chalky clouds
and listen to sound of the graveyard
and the headstones bearing their silent poems.

Bird call and leaf rustle are the songs
my father has become.

• *Galileo*

Finished at last: his tube of plain brass
tipped at each end
with a hand-polished miracle.

He stepped out into the Venetian night.

Saturn spinning like a child's toy.
Jupiter candled with moons. What
the hell?

He took a firm grip on the bar,
braced himself, and levered Earth
out to the dark edges. Simple.

Now it was just a matter
of prying the sun into the middle...and

presto! There you go.
It was surprisingly easy.

Best of all, the Pope would flip out,
a brass rod rammed up his pious ass.
What a night he was having!
Plus, he had just discovered the universe.

But it was getting late.
He put down his telescope
and went inside, moving carefully.
Christ, it was dark in there.
All he needed was to knock something over
and wake up Marina, who had long since
lost patience with his wee hour vigils.

She liked early nights, dining at home.
His inventions, his experiments with gravity,
the starry glitter of the court—who needs it?

But she was quick to laugh, and in bed
a great inventor. He eased in beside her.
I will never understand this woman, he thought.

• *Transitions*

Eugene and Clara, my Jehovah's Witness neighbors,
asked me to keep an eye on their house this weekend.
They have to go to Philadelphia
to attend the funeral of Eugene's uncle,
who transitioned last week.

I'm not sure if that's a black thing
or a Jehovah's Witness thing, or what,
but in any case I'm willing to give it a try.
Maybe death, like a lot of other words—
fat, retard, spinster—has used up its shelf life.

I'll admit, I never cared for it.
It's an unfriendly, no-nonsense sort of word.
It's just so limiting.
Whereas *transitioned* has a positive, forward-thinking quality,
like moving up from Bear to Life to Eagle Scout.
Like climbing the corporate ladder.

It makes me miss my aunt
and the conversation we would have had
over coffee and scrambled eggs,
exploring the possibilities:
Insurgents Demand Transition to America.
Domestic Dispute Results in Transition.
Serial Killer Gets Transition.
And so forth.

Yes, there'd be some awkward moments:
Till transition do us part, or
You darned kids will be the transition of me.
Worst of all, *Transition, be not proud.*

But now my aunt has herself transitioned,
and these words just hover in the air,
the changed and empty air
her laughter would have filled.

• *Fair Warning*

Suddenly my gutter fell off with a loud bang.
I looked into the backyard and there it lay,
bent and defeated among snowdrifts.

I could have said, *suddenly and without warning,*
but that would not have been true,
as there had been warnings aplenty. First,
the ominous overflow when the thaw came last week.
Water was pouring over the gutter,
not passing cooperatively along its aluminum canal.
But I felt no alarm, such is my sense
of being somehow set apart from ordinary human concerns.

Second, last fall
several people came by my house—
gutter cleaners and/or experts—
to look at my clogged gutters and give fair warning.
I attract experts in all fields—legal,
automotive, dental, marital. They offer the phrase,
"If you don't take care of that pretty soon,
you're going to be screwed," or some variation thereof,
which I seldom heed. In support of this
I have quite a few stories I tell at parties
involving root canals, divorce,
getting the "boot" placed on my car, etc.

Ah, the experts.

And yet...and yet...

My ex-wife is happy and prosperous.
I'm happy with my new tooth. And the snow melts
and drips from the unguttered roof, running off
to nourish the lawn and the bushes,
making me wonder if there was ever a need
for these gutters in the first place.

• *A Perfect Day*

It was one of those days
when my ducks were in a row,
for whatever reason. The mare
of night had galloped around
in somebody else's head for once,
and there were no ants in my pants.

None of my chickens had come home to roost.
Not one. Almost unheard of,
if you know anything about chickens.
There was something fishy about it.
Maybe they had me buffaloed,
but this time my dog days were barking
up the wrong tree. My fettle was the cat's meow.

Yes, there was an elephant in the room,
the white one. But for once
it wasn't an albatross around my neck.
Even the five-hundred pound gorilla seemed cowed.
I played possum till the cows came home,
then went out and milked my cash cow.
I squirreled away the cash.

If there was a stool pigeon in the vicinity
or a snake in the grass, he wasn't going to rat on me.
Not in a pig's eye, he wasn't. Although I had a goat,
there was nothing to get it.

It was one of those days
when you feel like your belfry
has probably seen its last bat,
your bonnet its final bee.

Of course, the turtle was still crawling
at a snail's pace. And on a wall somewhere,
someone was a fly. But it wasn't me.
I was free as a bird. I smiled wolfishly
and felt my oats. As did you.
And we made like bunnies.

• *Red Bud*

At McDonald's franchise #3135,
according to the sales receipt,
my aunt and I stop for a coke.

We are in Red Bud, Illinois,
according to the receipt,
and it is on July 23 at 3:17pm
that we each purchase 12oz. of diet.

We're down here to visit the grave
of my great-great-grandfather,
who arrived from Austria in 1850,
leaving Europe in a mess.

He married a woman he met on the boat
and they walked around in a dream, speaking German
on the all-natural bosom of the New World.

Europe would have to get along without them.

With his horse and plow
he was a dust cloud in the kitchen window.
She loved to stand there and stare
at the nineteenth century, not far

from franchise #3135,
where behind the counter
a kid named Dale,
with personal issues and incredible acne,
dreams of leaving Red Bud.

• *Solstice*

It's June, and out on the sidewalk
the girls are trying out their newfangled breasts,
just to see if the darned things actually work,

stretching, pirouetting for the boys
who are practicing smoking
in front of the deli,

as a couple of women, *nouveau obese*,
look up from their pecan rolls and fail
to vaporize them with a glance.

Everyone's singing elegies for spring,
and there's a light snowfall

of cottonwood seeds overhead.
Hardly a chance in a million
any one of us will get what we want,

but the seeds sail gaily overhead
with their cargo of unrealistic expectations,
as the grownups on the patio

mutter into cell phones.
Their kids were supposed to launch
the revolution today, but then

they forgot. And somewhere,
several dark unshaven men
pore over drawings of a mall
or an airport. It would be nice,

they're thinking, to blow something up,
with maximum loss of life,
but not today.

As for me, I think I'm caught
in that held breath between being older
and being old.

There's a warrant out for me
for everything I never did
but wanted to,
back when there was time.

Oh well, I think,
glancing at my watch
and at the sun, about to touch down
on the last of our lengthening days—

maybe there still is.

• *The Autumn House Poetry Series*

Michael Simms, General Editor

Snow White Horses by Ed Ochester
The Leaving, New and Selected Poems by Sue Ellen Thompson
Dirt by Jo McDougall
Fire in the Orchard by Gary Margolis
▲ *Just Once, New and Previous Poems* by Samuel Hazo
The White Calf Kicks by Deborah Slicer • 2003, selected by
  Naomi Shihab Nye
The Divine Salt by Peter Blair
▲ *The Dark Takes Aim* by Julie Suk
Satisfied with Havoc by Jo McDougall
Half Lives by Richard Jackson
▲ *Not God After All* by Gerald Stern (with drawings by Sheba Sharrow)
Dear Good Naked Morning by Ruth L. Schwartz • 2004, selected by
  Alicia Ostriker
▲ *A Flight to Elsewhere* by Samuel Hazo
Collected Poems by Patricia Dobler
The Autumn House Anthology of Contemporary American Poetry
  edited by Sue Ellen Thompson
Déjà Vu Diner by Leonard Gontarek
lucky wreck by Ada Limón • 2005, selected by Jean Valentine
The Golden Hour by Sue Ellen Thompson
Woman in the Painting by Andrea Hollander Budy
Joyful Noise: An Anthology of American Spiritual Poetry
  edited by Robert Strong

No Sweeter Fat by Nancy Pagh ● 2006, selected by Tim Seibles
Unreconstructed: Poems Selected and New by Ed Ochester
Rabbis of the Air by Philip Terman
The River Is Rising by Patricia Jabbeh Wesley
Let It Be a Dark Roux by Sheryl St. Germain
Dixmont by Rick Campbell
The Dark Opens by Miriam Levine ● 2007, selected by Mark Doty
▲ *The Song of the Horse* by Samuel Hazo
My Life as a Doll by Elizabeth Kirschner
She Heads into the Wilderness by Anne Marie Macari
When She Named Fire: An Anthology of Contemporary Poetry by American Women edited by Andrea Hollander Budy
67 Mogul Miniatures by Raza Ali Hasan
House Where a Woman by Lori Wilson
A Theory of Everything by Mary Crockett Hill ● 2008, selected by Naomi Shihab Nye
What the Heart Can Bear by Robert Gibb
Blood Honey by Chana Bloch
Farang by Peter Blair
The Gift That Arrives Broken by Jacqueline Berger ● 2009, selected by Alicia Ostriker
The White Museum by George Bilgere

● Winner of the annual Autumn House Poetry Prize
▲ Hardcover

• *Design and Production*

Cover and text design by Kathy Boykowycz
Cover painting: "Airport Motel" by David Wilder

Set in Century fonts, originally produced c. 1890 by American
Type Founders

Printed by Thomson-Shore of Dexter, Michigan, on Nature's
Natural, a 40% recycled paper